The Lost Thing

Poems by
Cynthia Linville

Chris —
So wonderful sharing
poetry w/ you.

Cover Photograph by Christian DeLaO

Bio Photograph of Ms. Linville by Anita Scharf

ISBN: 978-0-9846403-3-1

Library Of Congress Control Number: 2012934922

Cold River Press
11402 Francis Dr.
Grass Valley, CA 95949
www.coldriverpress.org

For my Muses

Acknowledgements

The author would like to thank her publisher, Dave Boles, as well as members of the *Sacramento Poetry Center's* Tuesday Night Workshop, the April First Writing Group and the Girls' Poetry Group for their encouragement and helpful criticism over the years these poems were written. She would also like to express her gratitude to her long-time poetry mentor, Dennis Schmitz.

Table of Contents

The Lost Thing

Cynthia Linville

Wandering Sunday, lost,

I found this garden
caught in the circle of the past:
time apertures here.

Heat is running out into night.
Chose the last memory fairly:
even the sweetest pilgrimage shatters
under too much light.

The moon makes me thirsty.
Venus whispers in my ear:
Go ahead, bite into the plum.
What is there to fear?

Heat

The sight of your red 4X4 truck
in the parking lot
draws me to you.
We smile, talk as good friends do.
I watch your lips move –
get lost in the salty smell of you.
You lean in close to my cheek to whisper
and the corner of my mouth
where you almost kissed me
still tingles hours later.

Leaning into the Wind

barefoot, long legs stretched beside me
you cross your toes with a sigh

a smile quirks at the corner of your mouth
eyes alight, hotter blue than the sky

expansive, your arms reach wide
your mask, a cheshire grin

your hands are birds in flight
inviting me to catch them

your three day stubble
invites my hand, my cheek

my tongue invited by
the slight gap between your teeth

my fingers itch to caress your scars
your knee, your side, your chin

flying, arms spread
I lean into you, as into a strong wind

Joshua Tree National Park

I watch bees dance in the shade of this desert rock
where fingernails of the gods
have scratched blood-red lines
and I think about your scars.
I would like to learn you by touch.
I love the stillness here:
a place quiet enough to hear each other's thoughts

but an obscure bird call teases us
a fragrance puzzles us
(sage mixed with desert thyme?)
and all I can think about is
the jalapeño slice you carefully quartered
and placed on my tongue
one bite at a time.

I want to climb inside your skin
curl up next to your heart
ride the slow-wave of blood
rushing in
rising without crest.
Somewhere the future has already happened –
I just don't remember it yet.

Aperture

I open wider and wider
to admit your light.

High Church

at weddings and funerals
you deeply inhale the incense
but don't hear the words:
you just go home to tend your shrines

boxes of teeth, animal bones
feathers, shell, bits of stone,
unraveled fabric of favorite clothes long gone:
you are an instinctual shaman

each morning you visit the boneyard
of your ancestral altar:
a perfect line of fishing rods
bequeathed to son from father

hunting and fishing an excuse
to visit your sacred places:
the San Francisco Peaks
the Anderson Mesa

such rites soothe troubled ghosts
you offer up prayers,
sage smoke:
your campsite, a kiva

Small Craft Warning

the hair on my arm rises
in response to your electricity,
I lean in closer
smell fresh fish
pleasant on your skin
sea-breeze in your hair;
your breath whispering in my ear
drowns out your words
as the ocean-roar of my heartbeat
drowns out mine

Kissed By Venus

I sink under
panic
taste foamy tears
and hair
claw at slippery seaweed
lose my grip
bang my knee on a rock
barely feel it
grabbed by the riptide
pulled out
under
down
panic again
and then
I stop struggling
and open my mouth.

This is a day where the perfect sky

comes right down to the sand
creating a private island.

Even the gleeful shouts
of children splashing fade out
when we lace our fingers.

Because I can barely stand
the radiance of your face
I have to turn away.

Questions gather
then slip through my hands
in a susurrus of sand.

I inhale – *here*
exhale – *now*
breathing with the waves.

Maybe next time I'll ask for rain.

I chose you

and I cannot un-choose you
even now that you are only the afterburn
of an image: a vertical line on the horizon
your lanky arm raised tall
in a salute goodbye.

I chose you
yet I could not choose for you
even as you lay shivering
fragile as a bird
after your fall from grace
onto the featherbed of my body.

Night after sleepless night
I wrestled with the choosing,
yet at dawn
I always reached for you.
I would choose you again
if I could.

This is the place we last stood together hand in hand

I can still taste our loss in the briny air
Why did I come back here?

The place where long ago you stood behind me on
    summer nights
your hands resting lightly on my shoulders
your lips just brushing my neck

The place where later
helpless in our arguments
we held onto each other for balance

The place where our lives
broke in slow motion and
slipped off this balcony into the sea.

Pilgrimage to Duncan's Landing

Lush pastures roll out
wildflower-patch quilts
as eye soothing sheep flow
past my window,
the eucalyptus and manure scented air
blows in,
and then
(I'm almost there)
misty brine,
and the guilt and loss I carry
tastes like sand in wine.

At the overlook
salt-laced wind slaps my face
as the tide's thunderous rage
chews the cliff scape
inch by inch
into new shapes,
as the years have chewed
my inner landscape.
I climb down barefoot
to pace a gentler beach:
this briny repository of secrets

I've doled out slowly over the years –
a lover in jail
the death of a friend
the beginning of an affair
the end of an end –

these resilient waves never fail to soothe me
with their sibilant liturgy:
pardon
and peace
pardon
and peace.

At night the sharp stars
sting
like grit in my eye
and the surf's soft caress
sounds like your absence –
breathing in
breathing out
breathing in –
while the cant of foghorn
absolves me
of every sin.

Santa Cruz Beach Boardwalk

As we wind down 680 and 17
we three talk work and relationships
offering solace and perspective
as only friends of twenty years can:
bankruptcy, divorce, and thorny coworkers
shrink in size
when viewed beside
well-worn college stories
of delectable sins
(for a while, we are twenty again).
We catch up
on the death and success
of people we knew
until the sea comes into view.

After twelve summers
of annual visits
we know the route by heart:
turn left to buy the wrist bands
ride the Tsunami
the Tornado
the Crazy Surf twice
(for Joy once will suffice)
our nostrils assaulted
by smells that grow stronger
as the day wears on:
sticky funnel cakes, Coppertone,
garlic fries, diesel fumes,
rank fish, and vomited beer.

Sally, the cultural critic,
points out amusing signage
(*Condiments* on an arrow
pointing to a trash can)
while Joy, the naturalist,
examines the multicolor geraniums
unfurling ferns, perfect spider webs
and I, the hedonist,
lose myself in teenage memories
of boys' fumbling mouths and hands
out on the sand.

Aiming for the horizon

I wade calf-deep
in the thin mist that the waves
breathe over the sand,
walking as far south as I can
past the family picnickers
the surfers
the driftwood sculptures,
past the footbridge that leads over the dunes.
(That bridge leads to the house
where Charlie Beck kissed me in the kitchen
the summer I was 15.)
I walk until exhausted.
I walk until the tide forces me back.
A ship on the horizon
matches my pace for a mile
then pulls on ahead.
The surfers and picnickers have gone home
and my outbound tracks
have been erased.
The water's foamy kiss is colder
as I lean down,
pick up a green-veined rock.
Back in the parking lot
a man stands on a picnic table
holding a sandwich above his head
in offering
to a flapping cloud of gulls –
a gesture so ancient
it inspires me
to stand at the cliff's edge
and throw my rock
back into the sea.

Meditating in Yoga Class

I pretzel my creaking body
into Upavista Konasana
and am surprised by
the sweet smell
of slick hardwood
and the memory of
my jazz shoes flying
across this same floor
twenty years ago,
lifting me in *grand jetés, piqués,* and pirouettes
my artfully tattered leotard
drenched in sweat
as I show off
for the dance captain
by the hour.
Today
the mirrored warmth of the room
overwhelms me
with that same lust:
impossible
elusive
yet as pervasive
as dust.

Me and Us and You

I wake up disoriented, back in the bedroom I had when I was 15, with pastel curtains I used to hide behind at night, watching Buddy across the street (the one who lost his front teeth in a fight) make out with his girlfriend, slowly and with skill

> back when I used to sneak out to watch the garage band practice next door, and the guitar player (who looked like Peter Frampton) would pull me up on his lap for Bacardi-kisses and sips of spiked lemonade.

I wake up with a jolt to a world where even Peter Frampton is old and am overwhelmed with the thought: *I miss you.*

But which *you*? Surely not the guitar player whose name I can't remember, nor any of the beautiful boys (equally nameless) who paraded through my youth.

Who is it exactly that I miss? Maybe my young self so full of sex. But no, it is an *us* that I miss, a *you* that completes the *us*.

Perhaps it is the most recent *you* who escaped my grasp, or the *you* I wanted but never had. Perhaps the specific *you* is unimportant, but instead is a collective, all the *you*'s that completed me.

> Perhaps none did.
> Perhaps that is where the longing comes in.

Nevermore

(after *Nevermore, O Tahiti* by Paul Gauguin)

Staring off into the joy-suffused light
wearing your hair in long dark braids
you could have stepped out of a Gauguin painting
instead of my past –
26 years since the end of high school.

I disagree when you say,
"We are all refugees from the past."
Pasts like ours (filled with wooden crosses
and beatings in schoolhouses)
require a greater escape velocity
than other pasts do. You nod

the sorrow in your eyes so deep
I lean in for a closer look
and see myself mirrored there
in this crazy light.
Your pupils open wider and wider
spilling into the deep brown of your irises
pulling me in.

The Dead Kennedys: Bleed for Me
(Sacramento, 1984)

When I hear that song I smell clove cigarettes
and feel hot, rough pavement on my bare feet
scrounging for nickels in the street
across from the Fortune Teller's house,
or I feel the basement-chill on my skin:
orange crates and a blanket
pornos on TV and fifteen-year-old Skate Punks
boys questioning me,
comfort in numbers at eighteen
when I wore ripped clothes and cried
   black eyeliner, a lot
I slept in a closet then (no lock).

When I hear that song I'm back
   with the cockroaches
hungry and scared in the dark
climb in the window 2am
drink aftershave-tasting-gin
and fall drunk-asleep on the floor
   amidst other shivering bodies
black clothes and eyes
safety-pinned ears and hearts.
That song, and I hear the morbid giggles
that C Street park
harboring hundreds of the frightened,
   the angry: all marked
spray-painting our pain.

When I hear that song I want to forget Johnny
smiling on acid
cutting his arms with a razor blade
double-edged blue
(won't let me. . .
all I can do is watch)
and that bike-growling-ride in the night-rain
full moon and no stars
(let me off here)
his skull tattoos,
long black trench coat covering all the scars.

Here you are on a Sunday morning

(after all these years)
eating pancakes at Carrows;
you whom I almost married
(the evidence must still exist somewhere:
bridesmaids dresses hanging in closets, cake
order, ring style, sanctuary reservations)

forcing remembrance
of the way-back-then-high-school me
when I wore my hair straight and brown, and
wore nylons, heels and lots of mascara;
when you and I held hands in church every Sunday
    and
rode around in your '68 (or was it a '67) blue
Mustang (1BADMTG), my name painted on the
    door.

forcing remembrance
of two Senior Ball portraits
each identical except for the embracing couples:
one of you and me,
one of him and her. He and I were in white
and would have looked so nice together,
whereas you and I almost clashed.
I remember wanting way-back-then to paste
he and I together into one photo
and throw you away. Funny how, even before
  the Ball,

he always wore white
in my mind, and eventually did rescue me

in his dirty yellow Pinto with the dented door
(I had to climb in through the window).
And here I am now, almost seven years later,
    eating my eggs.
You and I sidelong glance each other,
just sit, letting the tension build.

My hair is short and red now,
and I'm wearing comfortable black
(on my way to a backstage theatre job).
And he (whom I left you for all those years ago)
is here with me. You
(furniture store manager) still look the same,
and you sit with your blonde Barbie-doll wife and
    in-laws –
all wearing pastels, fresh from church.

After I've finished mopping up my egg yolks with
    english muffin,
I walk towards you; he leaves to pay the bill.
Forced smiles and hello-how-are-you-how've-you-
    been's:
then, "I married him last December."
And you, "Yeah, I heard." And now
over greasy bacon and sticky
orange juice, no more
guilt. And I leave you,
again.

Your eyes make me thirsty,

you used to say, *root beer eyes.*
I have loved your lyrics all my life
but I am nearly knocked to my knees today
by this faded pink note
tucked away in this dusty book –
Your eyes are pretty even when they're closed –
a note from an era when
your music shook my core.
but I'm not your wife
anymore.

Love's Labours Lost

You are standing in my bedroom doorway
with crooked nose and grin.
Surprisingly, you are 17
with bare, muscular arms
(football arms) and
a full head of dark curly hair;
then suddenly
you are 29
fatter in the middle
thinner in the hair;
then 45,
the years heavier still.
You must be a trick of light
or of memory –
you are not here at all.
(You are long gone.)
Only the doorway is the same.

Like Lot's Wife, I Look Back

"You are blind," she says. But all I can see are the unmarked suitcases I lost long ago at the cross-roads where everything I said was the wrong thing, where his enameled rejection left me beat-up, spiraling.

"Karma," she says, as if that explained everything. As if that explained anything. As if that explained the loss of his naked hands, the loss of a smile I could drown in.

This I see: This once-lush landscape is now a desert, but I am not a pillar of salt. This can again become a sea.

Inventing Love

I wake up to find my fingers
twisted through your long hair
and your arm tight around me
and the stereo going on, then off
then on again in the storm.

I'd been dreaming of a woman
pacing round and round the courtyard
her boots clicking over
the heart-shaped stone
near our door.

My mouth is dry
and I almost taste blood.

I go back to sleep and dream of an old woman
dancing naked in the rain
brandishing yellow fig leaves like fans
and when I wake again
I don't know where I am.

Then I remember that I heard your name
    in my head
before you even told me.

I have no map
for this new terrain.

Drowning Ghosts in the Park

dusk hangs between us like a confessional curtain
as I watch your rose-petal mouth whisper
across this concrete
bolted-down table.
I want to pull the dusk-curtain down over our
    heads
and giggle with you beneath it
because I can hardly bear
your sorrow and

our bare toes touching.
between us lies your unsheathed
Bowie knife
and the remains
of our Southamerican dinner.
your dread-locks hang down over your face,
    shadowing

your eyes
and as you continue
your lovers-confession to me, I
trance-like
pick up the knife
walk around the table behind you
and begin to
(gently sawing)
cut
ghosts out of your hair:
the Baptist-missionary father wandering
    El Salvador,
the male-lover dead to the bottle,

the drowned 2-year-old daughter
   you never even met.
you just let me cut
your hair,
you just let the words,

the tears
make me want to reach up and pluck
the full moon
out of the milky sky,
roll it between my fingers
like a grape, and
pop it into your mouth,
so there are no more
words, no more sorrows

instead I take your hand and lead you
on the muddy path,
(almost slipping)
to the nearby creek.
in the water we can't even see
our reflections
only enough moon
as I watch you
toss your chopped-off, matted hair strands
into the rapidly-flowing stream;
only enough moon
to see them drown.

Some things are worth waiting for

Nobody touches the moon,
he says, *not even you*.
But I dress in blue, reach high.

Finally, one dawn shatters the moon
filling the air with her obscure fragrance.
I catch a piece

tickle my fingertips across it
kiss the fleshy part so softly
taste it

slip it into my pocket.
Yes – the moon is good company.
I won't go moonless again.

You cover me like wings

Your breath skims over my belly
covering me like wings
Your texture snowing petals –
skillfully un-silencing Spring

You cover me like wings
You un-silence Spring
Your feathers slowly brush my skin –
Warm darkness blankets me

Your breath skims over my belly
snowing petals openly
You whisper words un-telling –
opening the moon in me

something unsung is mine

borrowed between dawn and never

so much of now
began ago

on days too short
below anything skies

rough winds shake
summer flowers into snow

your hand in mine
holds all these years

you hold on
you don't let go

somehow this moonless ride

into smoky night
peels dark memories
off my frozen thoughts
(how my arms ached
from holding you so tight
on the back of your Yamaha 750 that night)

tonight flawed dreams float in our wake like grist
(at seventeen we thought
it will always be like this)
now sunken skies grizzle
but cover me only
with dirty silence and ash
this hot thunder can't last

something broken is she

shattered by the dawn
like the fragment of wine glass
she finds between her sheets

morning corners her
smoking out borrowed lies:
a dirty silence
she tries to wash from her ears

blindsided
by the riptide of his cologne
she promises herself:
No more driving in one-hill zones

somewhere beyond yourself

three white dresses lie upon time's walk:
perfume, tea table, toaster,
stairs, spoon
litter your obscure path.
such travels texture all experience
now hands want
but nobody touches such stinging rain
(not even you).
now hands hold nothing
(nothing different from any Monday),
such losses presume the question –
dare already
begin again.

Shattering

The morning of the day you left me
I woke up dreaming
of the full-length mirror
falling off the wall.

Why was I surprised then later
when you started talking about
doors that open
and doors that close
and doors you just can't walk through?

Now I wonder when the snow will erase
your foot prints, and I remember
the first draft of the first poem
I ever wrote you, and I notice
the mirror reflecting
a fingernail moon.

Reunion at a Sidewalk Cafe

All stories are the same, he says.
He sips his white mocha
reaches for my hand
tells me his second wife doesn't understand.
We both know we were bad for each other
like too much wine
like too much chocolate
like a motorcycle going too fast in the rain.
All stories are the same.

I want that moment back

I want to un-miss that chance.
I want you looking at me like that again.
But the past is fragile and slippery –
a grape slipped from its thick bitter skin.

The Sweetest Fruit

A crow flies overhead, caws twice.
My grandmother hated crows
magpies, blue jays, and all manner of birds
who mistook our fruit for theirs:
fat black grapes with thick sour skins
and sweet slippery insides,
apricots ready to split,
plump purple figs heavy in the hand.
Why am I not surprised to find you
in my garden this afternoon
(did the crow foretell your coming?)
not surprised to find your tongue
delicious in my mouth as a forbidden plum.

I need this

a day off
an iPhone
a rain storm
red velvet ice cream
more time
another chance
your burning mouth

Rendezvous at Folsom Lake

midnight water dark and heavy
against our pale nakedness

your boat:
international territory

we wring joy from our wet hair
curtain our bodies in moonbeams

waves slap the shore
long after we stop listening

This is a place where time flows backwards

a hedonists' paradise where expert hands
rub rosemary oil into your flesh
and even the chocolate is good for you.

This is a place where July can come in January,
sun glistening on acres of nudes
dripping wet from the mineral pools.

This is a place where the moon follows you
   up a hill
and a bright star stands over your tent,

a place where cries of enthusiastic love-making
can set off a cacophony of yelps and howls
   all over the landscape,
turning a winter evening into Beltane.

This is the place where we float
   in each other's arms under starry skies,
the place where our breast-bones touch
   and we make a wish upon the future.

The Party's Over

The tri-color deflated balloons hung up
   in the tree branch
pull me back to the day it started –
hard, tight, foamy words in another lost street –
pull me back into the day
   she and I drew our lines.

You have already seen the whites of her eyes
he says, *stared her down.*
What solace is there in the clanging
   of barbed wire?
What solace in clinging to broken string?

Why do you keep coming back here? he asks.
The fireworks were over long ago.
The street is empty.
Let's go home.

Looking for a Wrong Turn

Driving round and round this dead town
not wanting to go home
I revisit all the old routes:

Taking the A Train Express Uptown to 190th Street
turning left at The Cloisters
left again at the Puerto Rican bodega
where we buy black beans every week
then up six flights to our overcrowded
    but rent controlled flat.
One time I walked all the way from Canal Street
(the entire length of Manhattan almost)
and tonight I wish I could walk that far again.

In north Oakland walking home
    from Ashby Bart at night,
living a charmed life, strolling through drug deals
(piles and piles of cash spread out on the stairs)
crossing splashes of red and blue
slipping past the crack house to come home to you
in the festering Victorian commune.

And all those country drives from Harper's Ferry
to Martinsburg and back again,
surreal snow falling into my headlights
like a fairy tale globe;
or battling black ice up the mountain
    to Garden Valley
winding up Lotus Road to our little corner.

Yet tonight in Sacramento
I circle round and round –
Arden to Fulton to El Camino –
repelled from going home.

The Last Road Trip: Imperial Valley

We've been here before.
We know the twists and turns
of this argument –
the ground scorched along Route 86
from the crash we witnessed last year.
The Salton Sea
ever increasing in salinity
(and dead fish)
result of unchecked flooding
from the red-colored river
that nearly destroyed us all.
The mud pots
where we've almost gotten stuck
so many times
spotted red
viscous, boiling.
The Algodones Dunes
(just west of the Chocolate Mountains)
which have frequently been a barrier
to human movement,
including ours.
Can it be a coincidence
that this landscape also served
as the site of desert warfare training
in WWII?
We never made it
to El Centro
again.

Lost in the Fog

Six o'clock New Year's morning 1982,
the mist so thick
we could only see a few
feet in front of us:
lost in our own neighborhood.
You got out and walked in front of the car
guiding us home.

Years later, we wound down foggy Highway One
sheer cliff drop on the right
almost blinded by oncoming headlights,
I followed your advice
cut my eyes to the side
keeping the edge
in sight.

All this I remember
as I wind my way to the coast
through a dark corridor
of redwood sentries –
you: not beside me –
the windshield blurry
the mist heavy.

Oncoming headlights sweep round corners
like a lighthouse beam
and I strain to see:
am I still on Highway 116?
does the turn come later?
I pull over, still confused
separated from you

A Thousand Ways to Say Goodbye

Canceling our summer vacation
Going to the movies alone
Skipping the family Christmas
Trying to make this new apartment a home

Not calling you at lunchtime
Not picking you up from work
Not buying the last book for your collection
Not being comforted when I'm sick or hurt

Trying to hook my own necklace
Zipping my zipper up
De-linting the back of my sweater
Checking for tags sticking up

Putting away dishes without you
Setting the table for one
Watching food rot in the fridge
because I forget I am living alone.

Snapshots

The hot blue of the sky and your eyes
the yolk yellow of the striped beach towel
and the deep red of your hair and beard
are so bright (even now) they sting my eyes.
We were happy in Kauai

and even the summer after,
the summer of farmers' markets
deep purple plums
and semaphores of laundry
flapping on the line.

That final summer
all that remained was a fleeting notion
we should fly to Hawaii,
and a deep craving
for juicy plums.

I came to the river to grieve

the sweetness
of last summer's plums,
but instead of grief
I ache with longing –
a desire of the teeth and tongue.

All Is Fair In Love

I have picked locks
listened at keyholes
made use of clever disguises

stabbed enemies in the back
dropped bombs
taken shots in the dark

burned bridges
switched allegiances
stolen battle plans

led sorties
shown courage under fire
and taken my share of the spoils.

**What should I do with all these
love poems now?**

    Shred them into confetti
    to toss at your going away party
    Torch them on the backyard barbeque
    Fold them into boats
    and float them down the river
    Set them free
    (wings flapping)
    to fly into the wind

Cultivating Thorns
for Cindy and Harry Hurn

This beat up tin bucket full of used nails
followed you from
San Francisco to Toronto
to Yorkshire, England
when nearly nothing else did
except a soft grey sweatshirt
a red enamel tea kettle
and the tome you wrote
(but gave up publishing
after only one rejection).

These nails –
retracted from our coastal love shack
ripped from our daughter's tree house
recycled from the rotting rose trellis –
anchored us to the separate crosses
we bore across continents and seas.

Thirty years later
I find this bucket of rusty metal
in a shadowed corner of your garage
after we bury you today
and I am tempted
to plant them along side you
to see what kind of tree
would grow.

A Brief Encounter of the Third Kind

I picked you even though
you were standing under a ladder.
I drew you down into this joy derby
this rock and squeeze.
Paradise flew around the bedroom
cawing, calling.
We sank in
until our bellies were swollen
with that hot blue smell,
until a clove red wind
clattered tin masks to the floor
pulling us up
from this curtain
of night hair.

Halloween Night in Tahoe National Forest

Painting on your mask (to blend in with the trees)
you unmask yourself, become transparent:
aquiline nose, high cheekbones melt and
(stubble and worrylines gone)
you become The Pan
almost, here in the forest.
Ex-army scout, you expertly lead the way.

With slipping steps down steep leafy ground
we find our knoll in the dim flashbeam,
stop, and listen to the night
barely daring to breathe —
we two, the only humans for five miles, you say.
Under this oak-canopy
you toss away dead branches,
smooth the dirt with your boot.
Then (we take off our shoes) I cast the circle
by incense and candlelight.

We hum and chant and sing together
our separate songs,
we hum and chant and breathe together
and in the echoes
we sing and chant
until our pulses drum together.
Beads slithering over, slithering over maraca
snake-rattles chills up my spine.
The spirits looking on must gather

just beyond our circle
(the white-painted boy, the old Indian guide)
in racoon rustlings,
almost giving glimpse of themselves
but not

except for the Shadow Woman
   who dances with me
to your primal conga drum, so big
she reaches beyond the trees, touches the stars:
snake-arms undulating, stomping feet lift high,
hips swaying with bear-like grace —
At first just my reflection, then separate
she comes alive,
beckons me into her Shadow World.
I am frightened and have to look away.

It's that fear that holds us here in this world,
   you say.

Lucky Mojo Curio Shop

She finds the unmarked entrance.
She's here because her suitcase is only half-packed
so there's still time, isn't there?

Divination by crow –
flying from the left
unexpected trouble.
(But all her trouble has been expected.)

The lady suggests Five-Finger Grass
Four Thieves Vinegar
High John the Conqueror's root
but insists she first decide
what (and who) she wants.

Her husband once said, *I'm not afraid of The Devil*
but she has an inkling he hasn't met The Devil.
She knows The Devil smells like moonlight
and cannot be out-witted with good luck charms.

Omens

walking under a ladder
stepping on a crack
an owl looking in your window
your lover's ex coming back

stabbing yarn with two needles
spilling pepper or salt
letting milk boil over
not admitting fault

cutting your nails on a Friday
opening an umbrella in the house
seeing a crow in a dream
telling a friend your doubts

getting out of bed with your left foot
a rooster crowing at noon
13 sitting down at table
a total eclipse of the moon

leaving a rocking chair rocking
giving a lover a knife
saying goodbye on a bridge
dreaming of those gone from life

a mirror or condom breaking
a dog howling after dark
a broken clock that starts chiming
nursing a broken heart

You were gone

before the pink chalk hearts you drew
wore off of my front stoop.
I got rid of the chestnuts
and shiny pennies
you left me.
I don't need
that kind of luck.

This Poem Is Not About You:
A Post-Break-Up Spell

Say your beloved's name backwards three times.

Box up every love note, every gift. Seal the box
    with a double knot.

Smudge every room with wormwood, mugwort,
    and sage, and sprinkle coarse salt over all the
    windowsills and doorways.

Stay out all night dancing.

Take a new lover.

Post pictures of the two of you, smiling, all over
    Facebook.

When someone asks about your ex, look puzzled
    and say, *who?*

You Wear It Well

I did not dress for suburbia –
I knew enough not to wear polka dots
to the moon-washed cross-roads
where we would tempt our blues-luck,
the nearly-washed-out cross-roads
where a Scorpio full-moon listened
to the susurrus of straws we grasped.
The Devil moved his hands slowly
whispered sex in Spanish
and complimented me on
my red, red dress.

A Minor Mississippi Memory

Past one-hill highway
Fred, you two
traditional blues

Fortune Teller present
tells The Devil to come out
on a muddy Indian highway

Palm, card reading
trio abstraction
duo blues

Don't – please go.
A train brushes the future
callin' "no baby"

(This poem uses the words from titles on the blues
album *past-present-future* by Myles Boisen)

Sunny's Too Tavern

She dripped red across four time zones –
nail polish, hair dye, ink, blood –
trying to stay ahead of the refrain
that chased her like a flood.

In Barstow a honky-tonk shaman –
fingers trembling on guitar strings—
called her to the altar
at the motel across the street.

She touched him as if he could heal her
his thigh-vein pulsing her fingers
slightly off-tempo
to the music in her ears.

In the morning they felt like two skeletons –
teeth on teeth when they kissed –
and she drove on towards Mexico
still listening for the music she missed.

It all started in Nashville

It all started with your blonde hair
whipping into my face as you turned.
It all started with the drape of your arm
across the sticky bar.
It all started with your fingers
casually brushing my side.
It all started with your smile
flowing over me like whiskey.
It all started with your smoky voice
singing about stains that don't come out.
Why was I so surprised
when it all ended
just like one of your songs?

Not fried chicken but bourbon

not The Derby or the Red Birds or Wildcats
but Bluegrass (and bluegrass).
The Commonwealth but not much of it
except for those who got rich
removing mountaintops.
Kentucky:
land of magnolia trees and road kill,
second cousins and missing teeth,
Hot Brown and *Kentucky mean*.

Drum Circle at Antietam

In northern Shenandoah Valley
women bundled up in dark cloaks
pick our way across creeks
and stubbly fields
with candle lanterns,
blankets, and drums.
No fire tonight
no incense
the cold darkness is enough;
starless, moonless fog blankets us
as we settle down
into a rustling circle.
Out come the wet skins
and soft thumps –
awkward at first
out of sync –
slowly catch a rhythm
sparking heat
until we begin to soar
and soloists break off
to wing us into a trance
of war whoops
that carry through the mist
to the adjacent battlefield
where muskets boom
in memory of the bloodiest single-day battle
in American history.
Those cold soldiers
dressed up in the past
must wonder
if time really has slipped
and this time
the Indians have come.

Great-Grandfather
For Leslie Lee Atwood (d. Sept. 4, 1972)

In my favorite picture you are barefoot
milking a cow in Mississippi
squat on the ground
with a hand-rolled hanging out
   the side of your mouth
gazing off into the distance –
California –
where I loved to sit on your lap
and eat the peanuts you shelled for me,
loved your pleas to
Come give me some sugar
your voice as scratchy as your whiskers.
My mother spent every summer with you
back on the farm
where rich black soil clung to her shoes
and the nights were so dark
she was afraid she'd gone blind.
You were up an hoeing the rows before dawn
home for a collard-green and fat-back supper
a short nap
then out all night
hunting possum and raccoon for skins.
Summers, the whole family picked cotton
   for a neighbor
(bent backs and pricked fingers)
for 50c a sack.

Such life was a mystery to me
as were the butter churn and solid-metal
    clothes irons
that rested on your California hearth
after years of hard labor.
Years after you were dead and I was full-grown
I visited the old family farm.
Your old house is still there
collapsed in upon itself
in a heap of weathered boards,
rusted appliances, and sweat-like rain.
Mississippi is a different country now.

Grandmother's Shoes

Your feet purple and swollen
poke out from under the hospital blanket

reminding me how much you loved to wear
  dainty shoes:
shoes with square heels, wedges, or buckles

shoes in white vinyl, black patent or red polka dots
but always shoes with heels.

You even wore heels with polyester pedal pushers
as in this 1974 Mother's Day photo.

When I show you this picture you tell me
high heels always make you feel pretty.

Saturday Afternoon Lullaby

The dryer hums
The wind rocks the house
The surf sings to me
The golf commentators whisper on TV
and I slip into sleep on the sofa

Waiting Room

How can an hour in a waiting room
seem interminable
when the longest human lifespan
pales against 35 millennia
of human births and deaths?
Yet this hour of waiting for bad news
is interminable
nonetheless.

I seek to be comforted by the knowledge
that all we know is terminal
that one day even our steel and concrete
will be gone,
pulled down and eaten
by plants and landslides
tides and volcanoes
and all our bones returned to dust.

Yet I am not.
I am sitting next to a friend
in a hospital
waiting,
waiting for the news
that will only bring
more waiting.

Paradise Lost

I awoke that morning smelling your
   Jean Naté cologne.
When the phone rang, I was thinking of the place
   where Salmon Creek flows into Bodega Bay
the feel of salt water, then sweet,
   then salt on the feet
and of the summer we practically lived in the pool
diving under again and again
reaching out to catch the silver spoon
   before it hit bottom
learning to hold our breath longer and longer.
Now I float suspended
buoyed only by grief and memory:
your dry cleaning long forgotten
   until after the funeral,
the day you finished painting the nursery yellow,
the scent of lemons and sandalwood,
iced Bacardi and pink lemonade
   on dusty summer afternoons.
(*How could you possibly leave me in August?*)
I worry that solitude may become addictive.
I worry that you will reach up and pull me under
just as the strangler vines pulled down
my great-grandparents' farmhouse
leaving no trace of what once was.

Sufi Healing

Prayer beads heavy in her fingers
she chants in Sanskrit
calling the angels around us.
Pink headscarf askew
she closes an eye.
Wherever she moves her hand
warmth flows through me
and suddenly you and I are standing
on a sea cliff.
There's no such thing as the past, you say.
A white bird escapes from your mouth.
Twenty-four crows fly out of my head
spiral around you
carry you away.
I know a storm has passed.
The sea is flat and brown enough to walk on
soft between my toes.
A huge rock on the horizon opens down the middle
revealing empty space.
The shell falls away.
Warm bubbles rise up through the sea
as a trio of fish jump high
and someone shouts *Jubilee!*
Come back, she says
her prayers rocking me
her hands buoying me.

On *Ecstasy, Calmness and Art* or
Where Do We Come From? What Are We?
Where Are We Going?[1]

Every time I wake up I am dreaming of you
you, the one I lost:
the one I loved full-length with frenzied hues.

Much flows into that textured memory:
that inadequately deep Gauguin moment
so tattered in the afterburn.

Our bold lines melted in a dark frenzy of
last plums, sweet flesh and tight concrete.
You were all toes, but we were fingers laced
    together.

Ours was the pleasure of breathing
surprised moment after surprised moment.

Now the texture peels away.
All that is underneath is gray.

[1]The painter Paul Gauguin said he wanted to "live on
ecstasy, calmness and art," and in 1897 painted his most
famous work, "*Where Do We Come From? What Are We?
Where Are We Going?*" which resides in the Museum of
Fine Arts in Boston.

It's not that I hate the color beige (or *that's art*)

One white boot lying on the sidewalk.
An engineered crack.
The couple at the cafe table changes,
then changes again.
People walk backwards
mirrored,
then mirrored again.
There's something about the way
a circle shadows in a crescent
a boy chases a bird
a raw peach
fingers of rain.
Women recline
in splashes vivid,
almost fluttering
in every painting I love.
Fever swim
sweet ache breathing.
It's Tuesday.
The moon is in Libra.

     * * *

It's Tuesday
mirrored,
then mirrored again.
A boy chases a bird
in splashes vivid,
sweet ache, breathing
an engineered crack.
People walk backwards
in every painting I love.

There's something about the way
the couple at the cafe table changes,
then changes again.
A circle shadows: in a crescent
almost fluttering
women recline.
Fingers of rain
a raw peach
one white boot lying on the sidewalk.
The moon is in Libra.
Fever swim.

    ***

Fever swim
almost fluttering
in splashes vivid,
mirrored
fingers of rain,
then changes again,
then mirrored again.
People walk backwards.
There's something about the way
it's Tuesday.
Sweet ache. Breathing-
in every painting I love:
a circle shadows in a crescent,
a boy chases a bird,
women recline.
The couple at the cafe table changes.
An engineered crack
a raw peach
one white boot lying on the sidewalk.
The moon is in Libra.

The Last Time

It all starts and ends here:
a stone stairway leading to nowhere.
I recognize the touch of his hand.
Ghosts swarm the skeletal trees.
She is here too,
arms folded back like wings.
A lone broom sweeps the cold path
where we once danced.
An owl hoots thrice:
just one more who betrays you.

* * *

Just one more who betrays you,
she is here too.
An owl hoots thrice.
Ghosts swarm the skeletal trees.
A stone stairway leading to nowhere,
a lone broom sweeps the cold path.
It all starts and ends here
where we once danced,
arms folded back like wings.
I recognize the touch of his hand.

* * *

I recognize the touch of his hand.
Ghosts swarm the skeletal trees,
arms folded back like wings.
She is here too
where we once danced.

An owl hoots thrice.
A lone broom sweeps the cold path,
a stone stairway leading to nowhere.
It all starts and ends here:
just one more who betrays you.

Reprise/Reprisal

I find you here at the lip of my opening future
driving me into remember.

Our tingling hours together
left no trace but delicious fear.

How long we wished for another again.
Yet now, I cannot think desire into my open mouth.

Someone has slipped bitter charms into my coffee.
There is no back. Only out.

***

There is no back. Only out
driving me into remember.

I find you here at the lip of my opening future.
Yet now, I cannot think desire into my open mouth.

Our tingling hours together
left no trace but delicious fear.

Someone has slipped bitter charms into my coffee.
How long we wished for another again.

***

How long we wished for another again.
Yet now, I cannot think desire into my open mouth.

Driving me into remember
left no trace but delicious fear.

Our tingling hours together . . .
Someone has slipped bitter charms
    into my coffee.

I find you here at the lip of my opening future.
There is no back. Only out.

Glass Houses

The July-scented storm invoked thunder,
rain tight like fists.
All our boxes dissolved into wet.

Now the years are slick with surprise,
the solace of confession, inadequate,
the prayer candles, blown out.

He had absolutely no business looking.
He wasn't a reliable witness.
We failed to retrace the map.

***

We failed to retrace the map.
Now the years are slick with surprise –
he wasn't a reliable witness.

He had absolutely no business looking.
All our boxes dissolved into wet
rain, tight like fists.

The July-scented storm invoked thunder,
the solace of confession. Inadequate –
the prayer candles blown out.

***

The prayer candles blown out,
he had absolutely no business looking.
Now the years are slick with surprise –

the solace of confession, inadequate.
Rain tight like fists,
all our boxes dissolved into wet.

He wasn't a reliable witness.
The July-scented storm invoked thunder.
We failed to retrace the map.

He Knows Enough (Just One More)

I am the unidentified woman –
only he knows all my aliases.

Destroy this memory:
there will always be a girl in a pink dress

whose fingers form a perfect heart,
whose wings beat back longing.

By morning the demons have all gone home.
Daguerreotypes ghost to silver.

* * *

Daguerreotypes ghost to silver.
By morning the demons have all gone home.

I am the unidentified woman
whose wings beat back longing.

There will always be a girl in a pink dress—
only he knows all my aliases.

Destroy this memory
whose fingers form a perfect heart.

* * *

Whose fingers form a perfect heart?
Whose wings beat back longing?

Only he knows all my aliases:
destroy this memory.

By morning the demons have all gone home.
There will always be a girl in a pink dress.

I am the unidentified woman –
daguerreotypes ghost to silver.

*Destroy this Memory is the title of a Richard Misrach
photography exhibit, SFMOMA July 2011. Many lines
in this poem were inspired by a visit to the museum.*

I am Fortune's ungraceful daughter

crashing a party she doesn't realize is her own
until the last dance.

The east wind that flew under your feet
  touches us both
brings me back to every sin I never committed
  until it was too late.

Now a flock of angry questions peck
  at my exposed eyes.
Where is my unremoveable memory?

Eden's fingernails open my mouth
to reveal nothing but a sea of bitter teeth.

Return time back.
Return it to me.

Publication Credits

The following poems first appeared in **Brevities:** *I am Fortune's ungraceful daughter; I need this.*

The following poem first appeared in the **Cosumnes River Journal:** *Snapshots.*

The following poem first appeared in **CSUS Catchword Collection:** *Drowning Ghosts in the Park.*

The following poems first appeared on **Medusa's Kitchen:** *Aiming for the horizon; All Is Fair In Love; Glass Houses; Grandmother's Shoes; Halloween Night in Tahoe National Forest; He Knows Enough (Just One More); High Church; Inventing Love; The Last Road Trip: Imperial Valley; Kissed By Venus; Leaning into the Wind; Lucky Mojo Curio Shop; Not fried chicken but bourbon; Santa Cruz Beach Boardwalk; Saturday Afternoon Lullaby; Small Craft Warning; Some things are worth waiting for; something unsung is mine; somehow this moonless ride; A Thousand Ways to Say Goodbye; Wandering Sunday, lost; Waiting Room.*

The following poem first appeared in the **Ophidian:** *Shattering.*

The following poems first appeared on **Phantom Kangaroo:** *The Last Time; Sunny's Too Tavern.*

The following poem first appeared in **Poems for All:** *Aperture.*

The following poems first appeared in **Poetry Now:** *Cultivating Thorns; Great-Grandfather; Pilgrimage to Duncan's Landing.*

The following poem first appeared in **Pulverized Diamonds:** *Drum Circle at Antietam.*

The following poems first appeared in the **Rattlesnake Review:** *I chose you; Lost in the Fog; Meditating in Yoga Class; somewhere beyond yourself; The Sweetest Fruit.*

The following poems first appeared in the **Sacramento News and Review's Poet's Corner:** *I came to the river to grieve; Reunion at a Sidewalk Café; You Wear It Well; You were gone; What should I do with all these love poems now?*

Publication Credits

The following poems first appeared on **Sacramento Poetry, Art, Music:** *Looking for a Wrong Turn; Love's Labours Lost.*

The following poems first appeared on **Sacramento Press:** *Here you are on a Sunday morning; Omens; Nevermore.*

The following poems first appeared in the **Song of the San Joaquin Quarterly:** *Heat; On Ecstasy, Calmness and Art; Paradise Lost; Rendezvous at Folsom Lake.*

The following poems first appeared in **WTF:** *The Dead Kennedys: Bleed for Me; I want that moment back; It all started in Nashville; Me and Us and You; A Minor Mississippi Memory; The Party's Over; something broken is she; This is a place where time flows backwards; You cover me like wings*

Cynthia Linville has lived in London, New York, San Francisco and outside of Washington DC but keeps coming back to live in her hometown of Sacramento. She has taught in the English Department at California State University, Sacramento since 2000. She is active in the local poetry scene, hosting readings and reading with the group *Poetica Erotica* as well as on her own. Cynthia served as Poetry Editor of *Poetry Now* from 2008-2010 and continues to serve as Managing Editor of *Convergence: an online journal of poetry and art* (www. convergence-journal.com). Ms. Linville regularly contributes her poetry to the *Sacramento News and Review*, *Medusa's Kitchen* and *WTF*. A music aficionado with a theater background, she is usually out and about supporting the arts.

Cynthia Linville's The Lost Thing finds love all over again, time after time, and in everything from sea-breezes to those nights when "the sharp stars/ sting/ like grit in my eye." When I read her work I'm reminded of Mark Twain's voice of Joan of Arc when Joan is asked if she is in a state of grace. She says: "If I am in a state of grace, I pray God keep me there and if I am not in a state of grace I pray God place me there." Linville resides in a state of grace, stays there and invites us into that state to share it in a lovely poetry she crafts with a sure voice and a total command of her medium. Read this book.

D. R. Wagner
Poet, Musician, Visual Artist and Lecturer in Design - UC Davis

Cynthia Linville's new book, **The Lost Thing**, is an eloquent testimony to love, mostly love lost but also an unquenchable affirmation of life. The honesty with which she views life is manifest in these words: "even the sweetest of pilgrimage shatters/ under too much light." She is not afraid to expose the intensity of her varied life under this light. Nature is an integral part of many poems: the "forbidden plum," the bees at Joshua Tree National Park, or Duncan's Landing that is a "briny repository of secrets." There is also the strangler vine that destroys her grandparents' home. In her last poem, "I am Fortune's ungraceful daughter," she asks that time be returned back to her. "Return it to me," she says, words that echo in the heart for many of us, and this book of poems is one to which you will want to return.

Allegra Jostad Silberstein
Poet Laureate for the city of Davis, CA

"And I cannot un-choose you" are the haunting words that open "I Chose You" in Cynthia Linville's new poetry collection *The Lost Thing*, covering adventures in lust and longing. Linville shows astonishing insight into the ephemeral nature of lust, one of the sadder aspects of love. Her work about hedonistic heartbreak is timeless and universal. We discover how big the poet's heart is as she describes the torture of memory and the youthful desire to encompass the world, to know everything, to be everywhere. "Aperture," a two-line poem, can be applied not only to sex but to all existence. How well she describes the panic of those "Kissed by Venus" - one of her apt titles - as well as [how] "this hot thunder can't last."

Patricia Hickerson
Poet and former Penthouse writer

I'm jealous that Dave Boles has gotten the chance to publish Cynthia's work - before Rattlesnake Press closed its doors, she was on my short list for a Snake invitation. Still, it's a pleasant surprise and an honor to see how many of her poems have been published in Rattlesnake Press publications.

Cynthia's work is a joy: clear, accessible, passionate, skillful. She uses rhythm and repetition to tell us about her longings and ambivalence - repetitions which are mantras that remind us that love, whether it's for a person, place or thing, ain't easy, and that it can be, in fact, a real bitch. Cynthia brings us vivid pictures of all that she loves, though - not just sights and sounds but smells and tastes and touch. This is a well-wrought collection, and thanks to Dave and Cynthia for bringing it to us.

Kathy Kieth
Publisher, Rattlesnake Press